In *Synchronicity: The Oracle of Sun Medicine*, Tureeda Mikell lets loose soaring compositions; and no quote is out of the question on this piano. She is our mother of the blues. Exposing peculiar souvenirs made into establishment sanctity or the mis-mythology of a nation; here is a poet who never surrenders her love for her people. She is the eternal revolutionary. All of our ghosts present. All of our sacred consistencies applied through hers which is the only language that light travels.

TONGO EISEN-MARTIN

author of *someone's dead already, Heaven Is All Goodbyes,*
and *Blood On the Fog*

W0115273

NOMADIC PRESS

OAKLAND

111 FAIRMONT AVENUE
OAKLAND, CA 94611

BROOKLYN

475 KENT AVENUE #302
BROOKLYN, NY 11249

WWW.NOMADICPRESS.ORG

MASTHEAD

FOUNDING AND MANAGING EDITOR
J. K. FOWLER

ASSOCIATE EDITOR
MICHAELA MULLIN

DESIGN
BRITTA FITHIAN-ZURN

MISSION STATEMENT

Through publications, events, and active community participation, Nomadic Press collectively weaves together platforms for intentionally marginalized voices to take their rightful place within the world of the written and spoken word. Through our limited means, we are simply attempting to help right the centuries' old violence and silencing that should never have occurred in the first place and build alliances and community partnerships with others who share a collective vision for a future far better than today.

INVITATIONS

Nomadic Press wholeheartedly accepts invitations to read your work during our open reading period every year. To learn more or to extend an invitation, please visit: www.nomadicpress.org/invitations

DISTRIBUTION

Orders by teachers, libraries, trade bookstores, or wholesalers:

Small Press Distribution
1341 Seventh Street
Berkeley, California 94701
spd@spdbooks.org
(510) 524-1668 / (800) 869-7553

Synchronicity: The Oracle of Sun Medicine

© First edition 2020 by Tureeda Mikell
© Second edition 2022 by Tureeda Mikell

All rights reserved. No part of this book may be reproduced or transmitted in any form or by any means, electronic or mechanical, without written permission from the publisher.

Requests for permission to make copies of any part of the work should be sent to: info@nomadicpress.org.

This book was made possible by a loving community of chosen family and friends, old and new.

For author questions or to book a reading at your bookstore, university/school, or alternative establishment, please send an email to info@nomadicpress.org.

Cover artwork by Chuck Hipsher

Published by Nomadic Press, 111 Fairmount Avenue, Oakland, California 94611

First printing 2020
Second printing, 2022

Library of Congress Cataloging-in-Publication Data

Title: *Synchronicity: The Oracle of Sun Medicine*
p. cm.

Summary: *Synchronicity: The Oracle of Sun Medicine* by Tureeda Mikell is a poetic-prose journey into sun medicine, filled with a plethora of questions for elitist patriarchs, political satirists, and those interested in interspecies communication—from "son" to "sun" or "joule" to "jewel," as in "Spell's Labyrinth." "The Oracle" alarms time that signs body's mind heart with, "What does love got to do with it, where is the respect..." in "Worship Warship," to political prose honoring the Black Panthers. *Synchronicity* connects scenes seen and unseen spheres with greater journeys from the profane to the mysterious that contracts taboos often interwoven with society's relationships to our winged cousins, stars, and ancestors trying to heal us all from the great beyond.

[1. POETRY / American / African American & Black. 2. POETRY / Women Authors. 3. POETRY / Subjects & Themes / Inspirational & Religious. 4. POETRY / Subjects & Themes / Nature. 5. POETRY / Women Authors.] I. III. Title.

LIBRARY OF CONGRESS CONTROL NUMBER: 2020931799

ISBN: 978-1-7327866-3-9

SYNC HRON ICITY

THE ORACLE OF SUN MEDICINE

TUREEDA MIKELL

SYNC HRON ICITY

THE ORACLE OF SUN MEDICINE

NOMADIC PRESS

DEDICATED TO MY PARENTS,
KATIE AND JAMES MIKELL

In every deliberation
the impact of our decisions
must be made on the next Seven Generations,
those faces
yet still beneath the ground.

NATIVE AMERICAN LAW
OF THE SEVEN GREAT NATIONS

Sun medicine is an antidote against oppression.
It is an act of resistance!

CONTENTS

III

V

CLASSROOM GUIDE

FOREWORD

Synchronicity: The Oracle of Sun Medicine intertwines the sensual and the structural energy of words and phrases, song, poetry, wild cries of ecstasy, and longing. As, one dreams the dream; then, as if by magic, somehow lives the dream.

Sister/her/she Tureeda Mikell, as Oracle, helps us to value ourselves through it all. The Oracle in this slender volume turns the slave monitor/colonizer's language on its head and inside out. We experience magic as she pulls us into the examination and critique of the meaning and mis-meaning of words and become a witness to the ways that she squeezes out and nourishes with her own juices the tiny bits of wonder they contain.

"English gives us a headache."

And challenges the demi-god that upholds the language:

"Why did the son of the sun worship with warship
Prey on those who pray for peace."

Oracle, in verse, lights up the Sun and seeks to wrench real relief from the church and "churchmen" (She see as the situs of blasphemy and its progeny), Tureeda wants to set us free from the pulpit and its pastors (pastures).

"Church takes land, language, culture, gold, minerals
In spells they call doctrine of discovery by law of a holy see

Make our covenant with heaven and earth, wrong
In judgments we cannot believe

Tell us,
The rise of sun's daily light cannot compare
To god's son who died for our sins and rose
From the dead and will return"

Synchronicity reads as lessons, part seminar, part dreamscape, a course in Us and the Universe Studies. Tinkering and analysis of words and their meaning is everywhere in this five-part course. Slight shifts in spelling produce entirely new approaches to our understanding of a poem or song.

Check out "Spell's Labyrinths: Double Talk":

Altar	Alter
Arc	Ark
Enterprise	Enter-Prize

"Why alter earth's altar?
Silence the Arc for an Ark?
Why douse sacred fire of every kind?
Who enters prize for this enterprise?"

Tureeda, as Oracle, teaches and guides us through lessons in life, spirit, and struggle. The layers of vision and understanding are made clear. In song, she shares all of this for us to see, and more.

From "We Document," little one asks, "What are we made of?"

Oracle responds,

"We are made of ashes, bones, homes, and seed
Dirt, water, star memories ancestors left
For us to grow on."

Oracle explains just enough for us to want to know more, to inquire more deeply into ourselves, our pasts and futures. "Okay, OK!. Go on, go on." We are happy to become "little one." We wait, try to anticipate the next verse, the song that follows...(read the book to see for yourself what follows. Hint... maybe something about extra-terrestrials among our ancestors?!!

It appears that some of these poems should be read aloud, others in silence and solitude. As we view the presentations, choices can be made and minds can change. There is much here for almost any predilection.

Tureeda the Oracle (one who inspired by the spirits, is a person or agency considered to provide wise and insightful counsel or prophetic predictions or pre-knowledge of the future).

As health provider and medicine woman, community gardener, and giver of hugs, from back in the day and since, she has openly "served the community."

Witness the patience it takes to work with and convince middle-school children, told early they are bereft of a voice, that they can create and publish their own words in verse, lyric, and onomatopoeia. The response as they see themselves in print!

Apart from its intrinsic beauty and power, it is my hope that this volume of story and verse gives rise to great exposure for the author. Perhaps this book will generate opportunities for Tureeda to share her wisdom and love with communities beyond the Bay Area, to college campuses, lecture halls, carceral settings, and local bookstores around the world and in our own Babylon.

DR. JAMES P. (JIMMY) GARRETT

is a long time scholar activist and was instrumental in the development of Black Studies along with major literary artists as Amiri Baraka (a.k.a. Leroi Jones) and Sonia Sanchez, he was a major contributor to the establishment of the Black Arts Movement. He is presently at work on a memoir of his social activism in the '60s and '70s.

INTRODUCTION

Synchronicity: Oracle of Sun Medicine is impregnated with sarcasm, questioning, humor, ancestral aliens, voices, and word play for days. It may inform one to take a closer look at today's society through trials and joys of trying to fix today's foibles, and synchronistic occurrences that may seem to stun the mind with recognition of a greater collective at work (i.e., "Synchronicity and the Bird" or "Preface of Three Women."

Synchronicity is a concept introduced in the 1920s by analytical psychologist Carl Jung (and later expounded upon in his 1951 Eranos lecture), which he defined as an "acausal connecting (togetherness) principle," "meaningful coicidence," or a "causal parallelism" (see *"Synchronizität als ein Prinzip akausaler Zusammenhänge"* (Synchronicity: An Acausal Connecting Principle), 1952).

Synchronicity offers insights into causal strains, helps us understand the onset of disease, and removes cobwebs that blur vision and denies the questioning of our inner nature's participation in the visceral arts of our sensual body's mortal envelope via the art of listening and receiving wisdom. The oracle forewarns and sees where our two eyes cannot. In "Forgive Us" or "Preface of Three Women," we consider how questions are answered and how the remarkable intelligence of the body responds to the collective unconscious.

In a 2013 TED Talk, Eleanor Longden states:

"Inner voices are a sane reaction to insane circumstances, not abhorrent forms of schizophrenia to be endured, but complex meaningful experiences to be explored."

Poems like "Spell's Labyrinth: Double Talk" came out of my countless experiences of hearing students (grades 3–12) creatively fumble homophones/homonyms: "Will joules perish in parish of jewels."

"Questions for SS" speaks of thoughts and feelings, religious guilt, and damage done to innocent inquiry: "Did you stop feeling and start thinking? // Did you stop sensing with your heart and start // Rationalizing with your mind?"

"BWYB News: The Goldilocks Cover Up" demonstrates that what goes unsaid entitles the "other" to implant ambiguities of criminalities under the illusion of inclusion, allowing the innocent to accept criminal behavior, and unwittingly act out under the guise of a "well-meaning fairytale."

In his book *Devil on the Cross*, Ngũgĩ Wa Thiong'o writes: "How can we cover up pits in our courtyard with leaves or grass, saying to ourselves that because our eyes cannot see the holes, our children can prance about the yard as they like?"

What holes are we leaving in the courtyard of fairytales for children to read and believe they too can walk in someone's home, uninvited, eat the food, destroy their furniture, and sleep in their bedroom?

This is about the politics of language. As in the poem title "Poly-tics" we see the Greek root *Poly* (meaning many) and *Ticks* (blood-sucking parasites). The politics of language moves against life; we constantly struggle amidst the forgetfulness of how all is connected and nothing is linear..

There are poems here that reflect epistemic and ontological values by which psychotherapist, psychologist, psychiatrist, and doctors evaluate patients, yet do not factor in the patients' cultural heritage nor blood memory within the diagnosis of "dissed-ease."

In "Nae Nae's Tweak Out on a Racist Insult," we see concepts that play with SAT vocabulary words given to Nae Nae's cousin, (a fictional character and graduate from Harvard with a PhD in Philosophy). She tries to rebel in an inculcated language that is not her own while the fictional church in "Steal Away Baptist Church" makes it satirically plain, essentially saying the same thing as her but within a different vernacular and sector of thought.

Civil rights warrior Fannie Lou Hamer offers a searing aphorism: "Memory is an insurance policy against loss." To contemplate, forgive, and be positive is one thing, but to forget is like the body ignoring the inoculation that will prevent the onset of disease.

May the offerings within *Synchronicity: The Oracle of Sun Medicine* imbibe you with the courage to stand in the light of the sun and receive your oracle.

TUREEDA MIKELL

I

Mustard seed muses
Miniscule memory
Merits mighty trust

MY SUN

My Sun,
Lamp of the world
I will speak for you
Though scriptures mask
Your testimony from eyes
That once knew your light
Watched you walk upon waters
Oversee flora, fauna,
Mammal, animal,
Bird, and sea creature
Obey your season's will,
My Sun

Your guard-in legacy deeds you
Master alchemist chef, cook,
Sorcerer of elements
You feed multitudes
Flavoring nature's seed womb,
My Sun

Why falsify your records?
Hide your light?
Cut circuit-tree
From in-no-sense eyesight?
Masquerading one vow-well
With I-doll sacrifice,
My Sun

Unclean spells stray from holy wellness
Creates hell for pathologic wealth
Degenerates generations,
My Sun

An icon reads
Think not I come to bring peace!
I come not to send peace
But a sword ...

Why destroy peace
In your wheel that is done?
You are the reason life
On Earth rolls through heaven
While
Greed eats away trees
Disconnects inner-Gs
Deviates gravity
Habitat for humanity
Erodes truth
Integrity destitute
Disputing life roots, they
Brainwash memory
Brand you secondary
Awaiting a messiah as though
Your soul-our light
Is not required,
My Sun!

Too many religious saviors,
Too many competitive death plans

Too many eyes look away
From your ray dance
To ray veer a rote man,
My Sun

I need not wait for your return
Your morning light never ceases
For what I yearn
You are my testimony
My sojourn
My life,
My Sun

You,
Not born of man or woman
You,
True light of this world

You,
My Sun,
Our holy read
Our spark of light
That never sleeps
In heart and lung
As we breathe,
My Sun,
My omnipotent one
Eyes will always rise
To acknowledge
You!

JAZZ

Jazz
Seasons
  Reasons
   Notes
Divides distance velocity
Sound
  Grooves round
Moves
B A A M!
Bee bawp
Doo wop
  Ooooweee
      Transitions
Missions made possible?
 Oh Yeah! yeah yeah!

Crusin' juice in fusion
Minglin' hidin'
Dyin' n' re-visin'
Leaves
Fallin' from trees
Swingin' in breeze
Going deeeep

You Dig?

Feedin' roots
Miles, Coltrane, Byrd, Bessie

Free Quincy
  Legs see legacy
    Frequently feel base
      Treble from
        Hiiigh to
Middle C
Tuning 440 into melodies
Epiphany!

Dogon see

Jazz IZZZZZZZZZ
  A Sirius
    Mystery!

SPELL'S LABYRINTHS: DOUBLE TALK

Sticks and stones
Break bones and homes
Take fish hook star from eyes

Altar	Alter
Arc	Ark
Covenant	Government
Enterprise	Enter-prize
Paradise	Pair-of-dice
Prophets	Profits
Sail	Sale
Worship	Warship
Pray	Prey
Peace	Piece
Sun	Son
Parish	Perish
Joule	Jewel
Good	God

Why alter earth's altar?
Silence the Arc for an Ark?
Why douse sacred fire of every kind?
Who enters prize for this enterprise?

Why did the son of the sun worship with warship,
Prey on those who pray for peace,
Set sail for sale of piece with pair-of-dice for paradise?
Governments profit
Gamble with prophets
Covenant of light

Will joules perish in parish of jewels?
Whose good is sacrificed for concepts of god?

POLY-TICS

It's a game that's played
A time that's weighed
A tick against the toc
The meaning is here
It's very clear
We're in a time lock

Of a game that is insane
A medium of many words
But I hope in time
In this rhyme you'll remember
What you've heard

Learn the routes and what pursuit
In the language you must take
Be very clear
Know what you hear
And the changes you must make

Subconscious finds
The child like mind
Takes in authority
Of a light destined in a plight
Of total mediocrity

By this understanding
That is so commanding
In the language that we speak

Many don't understand
What the language commands
And the roots that go so deep
Inside our brains
That mangles and stains
The whole of left and right
Destroying our visions
making unclear decisions
For the mending of our light

As time goes by
We wonder why
Things tend to be at its worst
People so demanding
With no understanding
Under by spelling curse

Spell a word
Cast a spell
Tic toc
Know the roots
Begin to pursue
The feeling of the lock

Know and see a lustful deed

Of a language and its plots
Begin to understand
What the language commands
In poly-tics against the tocs

COMMUNION

Had not been to church
In quite some time
Though I meditate and mediate
In my temple quite regularly

Last day of family reunion
We gathered in family church
And had communion in effigy
Of the lord's supper
But this time there was a difference

It felt different
It looked different and
Awakened some
Apathetic melancholy
Discontented prefix fixed for tricks
I had not seen or noticed before
Then I heard a voice of pompous passion
Speak from his neck
From the pull-pit
From a blind third eye
Weakened by televised visions
Incisioned for psychic frontal lobotomies
Word spells splitting thoughts

Then suddenly I was caught by visions
Of a pale blue-eyed drawn face
Dawning a thorn brace upon his head
Dying for our sins or senses, I don't know

But as this voice of pompous passion
Continued to speak
I could feel the fear and pain
In daily puddles of rain
Ancestor's blood-memory
Sustained through me
Whipped ripped rocked
Over deeply troubled waters
Fear of the white man's god
Terror resonating booming trepidations
Generation after generation
Never to be thought of as post-traumatic shock
Over time
Made docile to forget and forgot
Past and present survival
Riddled with archives full of
Communion
We receive as rotting flesh to vultures
Strange fruit on trees
Tarred feathered raped castrated
Denied human dignity
As evidenced by our behaviors today

Then I heard a colonized brother say

Take, eat of his body
Drink, this is his blood

That's when the deacons undressed
A large tray of white cracker bread and
Concord grape juice and passed it around
Pew by pew for everyone to take eat and drink

And *damn* I thought
Is this some kind of voodoo?

According to the book Muntu
Voodoo means *protective genius*

Then I recalled a book read years ago
Written by an Ethiopian ancestor
Describing his first encounter with Christianity

He wrote

Others in this province had told me
Of this new way of worshiping
As I stood by the doorway of the church
Listening
I heard the clergy say

Take, eat of his body
Drink, this is his blood

And that's when I ran
From the doors of the church
Screaming

These people are practicing cannibalism!!

WORSHIP WARSHIP

Churchman,
Do vampires and wolves mock Christians?
Or
Do Christians mock wolves and vampires?

I ask because the sacramental drinking of blood,
Eating flesh, resurrection of the dead, and everlasting life,
Are embedded in vampire-wolf culture.
Some have called it the worship of cannibalism!

To make my point,
I overheard a mother ask her 11-year-old daughter
While Christmas shopping,

"Which human meat would be best to eat,
    an old person or a baby?!"

The daughter's eyes squint, brow furrows,
She responds timidly, "An old person?"

"No!" The mother snaps, "A baby!"

The child's eyes widen in terror as the mother
Continues shopping for gifts.

Help me understand, Churchman.
Every first Sunday of the month,
The church serves Jesus cookies

And Concord grape juice in effigy
 of your savior's body and blood.
The PPP—that is, the
Priest, pastors, and parishioners, are then
Blessed and assured their place in heaven.

Bless, a French word meaning
To wound, injure, bleed or die, and
Yes, Jesus was blessed, injured, bled, and died
 So what do you mean when you say,
"Bless you my child."
"Be blessed," or "Have a blessed day," Churchman?

Is your congregation blessed to suffer
As your appointed savior suffered?

Do you recall *The Da Vinci Code*?
Did you watch this movie, Churchman?
Did you listen to the supposed French descendant
 of Jesus use the word *bless*?

Not once did she use the word *BLESS!*
Not once in the entire movie does she say
Bless you to her companion and confidante to console him.

I watched the movie twice to be sure, Churchman,
And took notice that
Those who did met with injury or death!

Coincidence, Churchman?
Who profits from this word?
What god-spell has your church conjured?
Why call your priest *Vicar*, taken from word *Wicca*
Meaning *Witch*, Churchman?

Judge not, lest ye be judged, you say?
God sends us out as sheep among wolves!!

Why, Churchman?
Why be spiritually illiterate, deaf, dumb, and blind?
I see holes in buy-bull courtyard sign, Churchman.
You want us to lay down sword and shield by the riverside,
While shot, lynched, butchered, and burned waft the air?

Accept premature death as key to eternity?
Kill personal identities, survival strategy.
Deny cultural memories marking the sensory,
Admit we have no past worth remembering.
Surrender peacefully?
Forgive molester, murderer, rapist?
Become walking dead,
Lobotomize our head,
Heedless lambs to slaughter,

Prey for Church of Nicaea, Fathers?
Call it god's will?
Born broken, saved for a better place, Churchman?

What monsters do you romance in this Holy See?

The meek shall inherit the earth and
Go forth into promised land, you say?

Will land promised be 6-feet deep, Churchman?
Will it be Armageddon, Rapture, Apocalypse?
Will it fulfill your carnal needs, Churchman?

Onward Christian soldiers, you say?
Hitler's army and the Klansmen
Were Christian soldiers!

What are you saying, Churchman?
Ark mit fri?
Work brings freedom?
The sign that hung above Auschwitz gate,
Where Jews arrived, forbidden to leave alive!
Freedom did not apply to them, Churchman!
Your Freedom supplied genocide.
Fanged bullets blessing countless sons and daughters of Mary,
Bleeding into sacred chalice, parishioners drink
One nation under god's freedom-beast,
Consuming blood-eating flesh,

Country after country,
Kingdom after king-doom
Like vampire-wolves.

Missionaries discharging arsenals of Manifest Destiny,
Absolving Pope been a dick,
No responsibility!
Erode deoxyribonucleic acid, genetic defense.
Shoot holes in Mother Nature's soil sense.
Fill with silly putty, Old New Testament.

Repent?!!
Sing?
Bringing in the sheaves, or bringing in the sheep
We shall come rejoicing bringing in the …

Meat wheat bread,
All sounds the same in our head
And who's rejoicing, Churchman?
Why love the enemy,
Forget our past,
Pay no attention to who's trying
To kill our ass, Churchman?!

Is your god bipolar, a bully, a narcissist,
A depressed megalomaniac?
Why does he discourage sex?
Is he hetero- or bio-phobic?

Why does he not want priest or nun to get some?
Why does he hate pastoral men and women?
Why are farmers, hunters, and fishermen discouraged
From use of stars, seasons, moon, to gather food?
Why call them sinners if they do, Churchman?

Book of Genesis reads like Life is the enemy!

In the beginning, your god tells Adam & Eve not to eat from
The tree of knowledge, 'cause it wouldn't be cool to know
The difference between right & wrong?

Is your god serious, Churchman?!

Defile backbone guard-in snake,
Family fruit tree trunk keepsake, because
Eve ate and said it was sweet, and
For this cause god banishes them
From the garden,
Blames Eve and evil is born!?

Adam, now scared shitless with guilt,
No longer trusts Eve,
Afraid to know right from wrong,
Is given dominion

Over every
        Damn thing
                Including Eve,

And what are we witnessing today, Churchman?!!

Global warming, franken-food,
GMO seed thieves,
Homicides, fratricide, genocide,
Child prostitution, human trafficking,
Water air soil polluting,
Ozone layer plant animal species diminishing,
U.S. government coveting foreign land water,
Mineral sustenance rites,
Living with the unacceptable,
Unable to judge vampire wolf dictator
From the womb of life!!

Say it ain't so, Churchman, say it ain't so!!

I recall Orwell saying a cause can reinforce
The original cause and produce the same effect
In an intensified form,
And so on,
Indefinitely.

Churchman, your destruction is too great.
That Adam and Eve story jacked us up!
Got to go back to our Native ways.
Back to Sankofa days, back to fetch it, Churchman.
Back to Nature's natural language roots.
Back to family life survival truth.
Back to understanding earth-stars cosmology,

Native American, Dogon Egyptian Kemet psychology.
Gotta get back to the Tree of Knowledge,
Tree of Life's twin.
Got to know the difference between right and wrong,
'Cause this deaf, dumb, blind song

Is not working, Churchman!!

Denied access to judge, reason, or infer,
We have tossed our pearls to swine!

We're going back to move forward!
Back to face Esu, the Yoruba's trickster
Found in the middle of Jesus' name,
After the letter 'J' was created by the Romans
From the letter 'I'.
Are you trying to hook us, Churchman?

Come on now! Y'all cold, Churchman!
And *who* wrote the buy-bull?

Yes, we're going back to worship the crossroad
  of Mother Wit good sense,
Not the crossroad of god's only son
Sacrificed for our *sins*
A Greek word meaning to miss the mark,
And what mark did we miss, Churchman?
The difference between knowing right from wrong?

Where ignorance of somebody's law is no excuse
Defined by your rule?

Are you messin' with our mind, Churchman?!!
Why would god give his only son to
Die for us missing a *mark*?

And what does the buy-bull verse John 8:7 truly mean?
He who is without sin cast the first stone?
Make sure your aim hits the mo-foe?

Churchman, who made up these stories?
Who benefits use of these allegories?
Do vampires and wolves mock Christians or
Do Christians mock wolves and vampires?

Why not honor Womb-man's sacred mount,
Burning bush, lawgiver, womb chalice
That has bled without injury since Kush?
Restore mother's rock, life's door, eternal vessel,
Humanity's gateway for rich and poor?
Why deny one another's word as daily bread?
Why must one be made honorable and holy instead?

What did you say, Churchman?
        God is Love?!!
What love got to do with it?
Where is the *respect* is what we'd like to know!

Love is just another word pimping vision
After kicking its lover's ass, Churchman!

What about the golden rule?

Do unto others as you would have them do unto you.

Can't be your sheep
The danger's too bewitching!
So, let us be clear, Churchman!

The god of wolves loves the hunt of fresh meat!
  The god of vampires loves the blood they drink!
    Which god loves to profit from injury, death and deceit?

Tell us, Churchman!

Tell us!

Groups, populations
Among us demand one thing
Treat others as self

LOOK AT HER

Bantu tongue
Ripped into a thousand pieces
Babbles on and on

Eyes disguise Euro lies
Colonize visions
Breaks looking glass
Scatters her soul search for light

Circle broken
Her token blows in-no-sense
As she walks and prays
In displays of *being saved*
Holy anvil cripples her feet
Hobbling through his-story

She Eve ill womb-man
Vultures pick clean her imagery
While missed-tree bleeds
Millenniums of memory
Honor left to die
No questions why

Stolen from heaven's earth
Immortality's worth

Sacred birth
Flies blind in constant search of
Maternal rights

Vicar of Christ provides
The Our Father
Proselytize
Warships sacrifice
I-doll's sense-less rules
Five sin-say-shuns
Prey for fools
Hear, see and speak no evil
Judge not, lest you be judged!

She falls into a bottomless pit
Without floor, net or rug
Marked lunatic
Drugged by a world of
Hidden tricks
Turned inside out
Upside down
Wrong made right
Sold by the pound
She hemorrhages
Unseen
In nightmares
She screams
Where few listen

Or see
In Babylon
In Babylon
She is Babel
Babbling on and on

HEATHENS SPEAK

They spit his blood on us
With words
That trouble our hearts

Took our land
Took memory away
From our medicine men and women

Took our children
So we can no longer teach them
The ways of our ancestors

Call us heathens

Say their savior's blood
Is our blood
Say he suffered
As we must suffer

Tell us to do good
And love those
Who hate and despise us
Say we will be rewarded in heaven
For this behavior that kills us

Once every new moon
The missionaries
Make us drink
Red juice and
Eat white bread
So we will not forget
Our debt
To their savior
His sacrifice for our sins

We never understood
And do not understand
What this word
Sin means

We love our
Great Mother Father
Earth Sky

We live by laws
Of the holy ring
But they call us heathens
Tell us we need to be
Saved?

I remember what the
Grandfather once told us

He said
When missionaries came
  To force their way of worship
    Upon our people
We notice their savior
  Saves heaven here on earth for them
  As it was for us
    Before they came.

FORGIVE US
FOR THE INDIGENOUS AROUND THE WORLD

We have sinned
Missed the mark
The mark of your teachings that kill us

We should be grateful to die
In light your god's word
And dishonor the heavens
We witness with our eyes

Did not mean to spot your knife that
Cut backbone snake from body's
Tree of knowledge that sees
Where our two eyes cannot!

Did not mean to smell listen or be aware
Of feet fin feather relatives warn us
Of coming fires storms quakes or tsunamis

Forgive us for looking to them for
Protection though they have
Saved us many times

Please forgive that which sustains our lives
Forgive us for being crippled by that loss

Did not mean to be aware of medicines
From flora fauna tree star seed reasoned by season
Forgive our ancestors who have left us this healing speech

Did not mean to dishonor your god for our
Great mother father on this earth in heaven you call hell

Did not mean to miss the mark
Of your consent or be un-great-full

This is our sin oh great learned father priest
Your guns hangings beheadings and exiles
From homelands have convinced us
Your god is powerful!

Forgive us for judging your Vicar of Christ
God-spells that tell us we must wait for
Your god's son to return and ignore
Sun's light return everyday

Forgive us for we are sure you believe
Your god is the only true living god
And everything that has provided
Nourishment and protection
Before your arrival to our lands
Is evil, born of Lucifer, your *light* devil

Forgive us the displeasure we see in your eyes
As we celebrate existence through ritual rites

Sow seed harvest dance sing drum and embrace
One another in the presence of nun or priest
For this too is immoral

Forgive us if we do not see or understand
Your god's love
Perhaps it was lost in translation

English gives us headaches

Your words remove much from our world
We fear anger grief and confusion
Will consume our children's future
Who like us will be forced to believe
This land is not alive and listening

Forgive the discomfort you see in our eyes
For anesthetizing our flesh with pipe or drink
From sacred trees that temporarily ease
Slaughter of our legacy

Born broken, according to your god's word
We have sinned missed the mark and instead
Eagerly await the fate of your father in heaven
That shames our existence on earth

Forgive us if we do not know how to deify your
Intelligence that chooses to house the likeness

Of your god's only son's murder nailed to a cross upon
Walls that conceal sun from sky

We hear your church say *Amen!*
Desert earth womb-man children
And bear witness

Your worship is a war-ship against life!

Forgive us

TAKE ME HOME MAMA

Beautiful Nubian child
Taken from cultural vintage
Sixth sense right – wrong lineage
Shifts intellect
Swoons her into nausea with
Dizzying headache

Mother takes her to the doctor
Thinks he can fix those
Hidden tricks

Except
Doctor's education lacking
Neural ethnic mediation
Does what he knows best
Prescribe medication
Yet,
Forgets to mention drug
Side effect could
Make her see things
That were not there
And do things she'd not dare do
Though authored feeling
She had to

Grandmother
Of beautiful Nubian child
Noticed this unusual behavior
While Mother was at work

"Child, why you crawlin' out the window?
We on the fifth floor.
You gonna kill yo self."

Grandmother takes child back to the doctor
Who was taught to mock her

"Leave her at the hospital for a short stay and
We'll check her out right away."

One day later
They visit their beautiful Nubian child
Dry mouthed, glassy eyed
Weakened by covert trial
Grandmother and Mother
Could not understand

Doctor advises another plan
Authorizes shock treatment
Mother and Grandmother accept
Without question

They come to visit once more
Their beautiful child so adored

To witness more dread and
Terror in her eyes
With a strange look
And sudden cry

"Mama, Nana, take me home!
Please!! They're trying to kill me!"

Doctor says
"You can't at this time, she isn't ready."

Grandmother and Mother
Struggled a long while
Remembering
The last words prophesied
From their beautiful Nubian child

EYES SO BRIGHT: BLUES

I saw him under a street light
On MacArthur Blvd. one night
His eyes were fixed on a site I couldn't see
Yet he seemed to be free

His eyes were so bright so full of light
Head held high
What was he looking at in the sky?

Face brown and smooth
Did not give a clue
About all the truth he could see
But I felt in my heart
If he were in the land origin of his art
He'd be a priest seer
Of a very special family tree

His eyes were so bright so full of light
Head held high
What was he looking at in the sky?

Being a lab tech, people were subject
To have their blood drawn by me

Every morning I'd go down to make my rounds
Upon the agreed salary

Doctors made the conclusion
Patients suffered delusion
But with that I wasn't totally satisfied
Cause the light psychic soul vibes
More than a trillion points of light
But to prove it to them as a Black woman
Was a useless fight

And there he was, this brown skin dove
Still looking with eyes so bright
And there I was with Vacutainer
Rubber tie and glove
About to draw out a piece of his life
When suddenly he looked at me and said,

You won't find it there.

A MOMENT OF SILENCE

It was career day at Mac High
Brotha rolls up in a limousine
Dressed clean
He's sporting diamond rings
On nearly every finger

Students in awe
Impressed
Ask

Man, what do you do for a living
To make all that bling bling?

"Guess," he says.

Answers come
But none correct
Finally
The mystery guest says

"I'm a mortician.
I buried three young men
Just about your age
Before I arrived.
You see,

Your death
Is my life.
Like Jesus' sacrifice.
You *profit* me well."

(silence)

TODAY IN OAKTOWN

Cost to live
Rises

Life values
Fall

Newspaper headline reads
5-year-old child dies
From natural causes

Elementary school's main door
Faces two businesses across the street

To the left,
A florist

To the right,
A mortuary

Advertisement reads
Our business is blooming!

Entitlement rules
Condemns visceral tenant
Fence, bars existence

FACING COLD FACTS

Sugar face wears
Ice white teeth
Eyes glaring
Nose
Flaring
Uniform of poverty
False flag
High titles
Switchblade smile
Slice and dice
Platitudes
Served on hot ice
Demanding you warm up to
Frostbite!

But we
Stay cool
And dig all
Jive!

CONCEPT'S PHILOSOPHY

Concepts volatile inept
Born of ego
Ergo a will power
Immune to critical thinking
Double seeking clones virulence

Polysaccharide coat
Deceptively sweet
Viral
Impenetrable shrewd deadly
Hard to subdue or forgive

Notorious ruthless
A jingoist warmonger
Manufactures consent
Insidiously while naiveté
Accepts volubility
Big talk!

Misanthropic misogynist
Dispossess innocence
Intuitive intelligence as
Feeble pledges allegiance

To Pontiff's dictums
Transfiguring sheep-ill into
Mercenaries of secretive
Self betrayal

Beguiled
Cognitive dissident concludes
Ignorance is strength.
Slavery is freedom.
War is peace.
Have faith.

Avoid visceral sense
Vertebrae's electromagnetic defense
Denounce all prophecies
Unless written in B.C. or B. C. E.

Analogy
Wasp lays eggs on Spider's belly
Consecrated room
Host doom
New world breeds
Concealed moralities

Ordains abnormalities
Consumes fatalities
Demeans life sanctity
Transmogrifies natural selection

Sites linguistic frames
Taming trope's inflections

Suppressing all realities
Other than its own
Refuting all rights
Other than its own
Negating all histories
Other than its own and
Censuring all indigenous wisdoms
Breaking circle upon circle
Including existence sown!

Patriarchal sky general
Absolves terrorist decree
Is covert tactician of doublethink speak
Demands use of synchysis
Disorderly placement of words
Designs social schizophrenia
If accused will decry
Absurd!

Condones hypocrisy
Thrives upon hyperbole
Dims light
Damn souls
Psychopathic economy
Demonstrates control cuz

They who blind the people's eyes
Reproach them for their blindness, foo'!

Oh say can You Seeeeeeeeee?

No?

Steal Away Baptist makes it plain.

STEAL AWAY BAPTIST CHURCH

"You ain't shit,
 Ain't ever gonna be shit,
 Unless you believe this shit right here,"

Pastor says pointing to his buy-bull!

"Fuck yo mind and yo body bitch!
 Believe this shit!
 What you feel ain't real!
 Yo shit is broken.
 Yo shit was born broken
 But the Lord got shit to fix yo shit!
 Cuz like I said,
 You ain't shit,
 Cain't be shit
 Unless you believe this shit, and
 If you don't believe this shit,
 Yo shit can't be saved!"

Amen, that's the shit right dere!
Shouts the Steal Away parishioner.

"Yes, Amen!"
Responds the pastor.
"This is show nuff the shit of god!"

Drunk stands, pointing to his buy-bull,
You want us to believe this shit
Right herenigga, this shit right here?

Deacon answers,
"Yes Lawd!
Cuz the buy-bull is the shit!!!"

Someone yells from back pew,
THAT'S BULL SHIT!!
                              And so it is.

MY PEOPLE

My people turned away
From worshiping
Their source of miracle
And magic done
My people turned away
From worshiping
Earth water wind stars and sun
So they could worship someone hung
On a cross
Now so many are lost
Deceived and made to believe
Guilt from another culture
A vulture polluting
Our well beings
With sights of
Non realistic dreams
Now too many cry
Because too many die
By sacrificial death
Worshiping lies

Tried to turn us from the sun
And memories
Of water fire light wisdom

Drums sacred hums
Trees holding seeds with
Enchantment and glories
Telling stories evoking magic
Sacred names
Bringing thunder
Lightening and rains
Lord of my laws my gods
My people turn from senses
Engraved by life's light
Where body was first scripture
And earth by heaven
Held scripts
To the laws of life
From water spirits
Smells and spells
Atmospheric wells of genetics keys
From winds oracle messages
Through soft breezes
From mother tongue sacred words
Connecting third eyes
From bird's seasonal
Flight messages in skies
And the naming of our children
For presence in their lives

From earth where gardens had worth
And birth was not

An ongoing pain
Where raising the young
Was not a fearful gain
Where life wasn't
Frequently visited by the insane
And maimed for and by
A chemically synthesized
Drug infested diseased
Murderous reign

Yes my people are troubled
Yet they secretly know
The poisonous snake
They fight each day
As ancestral spirits whisper
Whisper miracles and magic done
With earth water wind stars and sun
Where darken skins have sung
Fire light wisdom

As dark simmering coals
Housing souls
In spiraled rolls
Of rainbow lights
Seers of scripted sights
Yes my people are troubled
By what might have been
Could have been

Before we allowed them
To turn us away from worshiping
Earth water wind stars and sun
So we could worship
Someone hung on a cross

But this too shall pass

FIVE-TO-SIX-HUNDRED YEARS OLD

After funeral
Eyes look with suspicion
Ignore cordial intentions
Avoid eye contact

Perhaps it's my African dress
Gele' head wrap?

Outside church gate
Wind trembles tall tree
Spirit speaks,

> *What you experience is*
> *Five to six hundred years old.*
>
> *Go to Chinatown*
> *Buy fresh salmon*
> *Swim upstream*
> *You need strength*
> *New understanding*

I go,
Do as told
Buy fresh salmon
Chinese merchant wraps
He bows reverently
Hands it to me
Eyes look into mine
Then at crown,

Says,

> *Nice, so very nice*
> *Thank you*

I nod back in gratitude
Surprised
Leave market behind
Head turns right
Sees pink lavender sign
Read

'Palm Readings'

Spirit says,

> *Go!*

I thought,
No! I don't go to places like this

Spirit insist

> *Go! Secure your seal*
> *What troubles you today*
> *Has a past*
> *Five to six hundred years old*
> *GO!*

I swim upstream 16 stairs steep
To my left, a door I tap timidly

A young Gypsy woman answers

> *Hello dear come right this way*

She leads me into a room where
Walls and in-tables and coffee tables
Wear old black and white photos of
Ancestors she says passed the gift
Of sight and ear to her

Two velvet indigo chairs
Face one another
She gestures me to sit in one
As she sits in the other.

Reaches for my hand
I present with hesitation
Bows her head
Gazes into my palm and
From deep silence says,

> *What you are going through*
> *Is five to six hundred years old!*

DEVIL'S ADVOCATE

Chemically
And synthetically speaking
For the ignorance of
Human sense and worth
For the great scientific
Medical forefathers
Who have condemned
Many families for and from
The miracle of birth
We have mind body and soul
Altering drugs for your behind
We have medications, the mediation
To ruin and numb every sense or
Symptom of your signs

You don't have to feel or interpret
Your senses that are due
Because between us and
The television commercials, baby
We're going to show you
What to do
And if your worries pile up
And get stuck

We got
M.O.M, Milk of Mag,
Correctol, Dulcolax and EX-Lax
To relax your behind
Because on us
You can depend with Attends
And that's a name you can trust

And if it's sleep you seek
We got liquids, powders and pills
To literally make you chill, baby
Especially if life gets
Too cold to hold
Just give us the money
We'll take control
You don't have to be
Whole

I've heard the stories
Spiritual psychics say
That our soul sends and receives
With electro-chemical impulses
That sense with intuitive release
Don't be response-able for that
Trust me!
Trust me!

If it's high stress
Body pain, or sleep you lack
Take some Nitol, Sominex, Mellaril
Hell,
Take some Crack!

Drug addictions you say?
We have drug treatment centers
For that!

Say you have a pain in your head
Like two bulls running after red
Well we make thousands
Of chemical medicines
Most are pain relievers
Coming out every year

We have chemicals in brand name foods
We even have it in your beer!

BHA, BHT,
Aluminum ammonium sulfate,
Aluminum hydroxide
And monosodium glutamate,
Potassium sodium,
Formaldehyde nitrate and
Aspartame known as Nutra-sweet,
As well as butyl butyrate

True
Most are not water-soluble
Even though ninety percent
Of you is
But look at it this way, baby
We're doctors and scientists
We're not here to find causes

We're just here to relieve
Your symptoms
So we can stay in your pocket
With a steady rhythm

Oh, about that pain in your head
Could be from MSG
Or possibly even smog-related lead

But why don't you
Make an appointment
So we can have a look-see
Or why not take some
Empirin Codeine #3,
Advil, Motrin, or Allerest
If you overdose we'll just pump
Your stomach, run some tests

Why make yourself
Response-able
For understanding
Or knowing your pain
When it's us
The doctors and scientists
Who need your senses
To grow insane
Because you know
We're here to keep you
And treat you
In hospital cells
As John Milton knew

We'd rather not serve in heaven
But rule in hell.

HIDDEN AGENDAS

Why don't you play hidden agendas with me?
It's a game of manipulation that will set you free
Is an aphrodisiac of the mind`
It's the psyche game of poly tics
Of the very beast
I mean, best kind!

When you play this consciously
You win much better
You don't have to play fair
Down to the letter

So, what about those in-no-sense minds
You gonna run into them all the time

Come on, play hidden agendas with me
Baby, I got game plans that will set you free

There's one drawback not bad at all
Keep notes mental or otherwise
So you don't take a fall

Avoid being direct
Play weak against the strong

With this poly ticking, baby
You can't go wrong

I know, I heard you
Those innocent minds

Well stay away from them, baby
Cause they'll blow your mind

They're so direct
They don't go for show
They're into body sense and
Love of the soul

Well I so love hidden agendas
Come on, play with me and
If you play it right
You can do whatever in hell
You please!

Ha!

LIFE LIGHT REMEMBERED

We are soldiers on the battlefield
With life light in our eyes, said Sister Sonja.

1994, 23 years after volunteering
At the George Jackson free health clinic,
The Tribune calls, asks,

How many guns did you have at the
Black Panther Clinic?

How many guns?
Not how many services were provided?
Not how many programs were implemented?
Not how many doctors or healthcare workers volunteered?
Not even why we'd care to put
Into practice such a program
With so many hospitals in our community.

No, didn't ask any of that!
Wanted to know how many guns we had.

Not what illnesses or diseases
Most affected our communities
Or how often we screened for diabetes, sickle cell,

Or checked for high blood pressure, if at all,
Or
What may have been my specialty
At that time.
I would have told them of certain grains
To regain genetic memory.

But they were more interested in
How many guns we had.

Not who ran the clinic
Or what hours or days
Of the week we were open
Or
Who was our hero or she-roe
To set about such a task that sustain
Our health needs today.
No, the reporter didn't ask any of that.

They wanted to know
How many guns we had.

Black men and women,
Late teens to 20-somethings,
Volunteered to become doctors, nurses,
Pharmacists and therapists,
Completed homework between
Seeing patients.

Black volunteer staff physicians
Drs. Tolbert Small and Eddie Newsome
Developed methadone program
To destroy heroin dependence
Reverse curse of opioid addiction
Purposefully placed in our neighborhoods
To weaken Black power base.

We took vital signs,
Provided prenatal care,
Kept patient records,
Organized charts, med rooms, pharmacy.
Gave better care than Kaiser dared,
Held life light in our eyes.
Books, our bullets,
Educationally armed our
Right to fight through walls that
Imprisoned us as violent, drug-infested,
Gun-carrying, sex-crazed jiggaboos.

Kwame Ture warned ...

Education in this country makes you stupid, but what is worse, it
makes you arrogant in your stupidity. The revolution is coming
whether we want it or not! It is coming whether we want it or
not! We must be politically prepared for what is coming.

The revolution will not be televised
Not be televised

Not be televised.
The revolution will be live!

How many guns did we have?

We were soldiers on the battlefield with
Life light in our eyes.

We are soldiers on the battlefield with life light in our eyes.

NAE NAE'S TWEAK OUT ON RACIST INSULT

You say my hue
Is color of shit you wipe
From your ass then flush?
Then be forewarned mutha-fucka.

Black brown seed
Become the
Food you eat
Become shit
You betta release
Or
We'll blow your asses up
From the inside!

This is not a threat!
It's biology, bitches!

BWYB NEWS: THE GOLDILOCKS COVER UP

This is the BWYB News, Be Watchin Yo' Back.

The Goldilocks Cover-up! This just in tonight;
Goldilocks breaks in Three Bears home.

Three Bears charged Goldilocks, a.k.a. the Golden Bandit, with
illegal entry among several other crimes implicated early Tuesday morning.

Witnesses say the intrusion took place just after the family left for a walk
in the woods. It was stated, when Golden Bandit knocked on the door,
and no one answered, she let herself in. Moments after alleged entry,
a witness on the wing said, quote,

"I saw Bandit steal and consume Bears' food, vandalize the furniture,
and sleep in Baby Bear's bed." Unquote.

Investigators confirmed strands of blonde hair found in baby bear's bed
did match that of Golden Bandit. Further investigations proved that
the fried chicken, cornbread, sweet potatoes and collard greens found
on soiled clothing of Golden Bandit was indeed taken from Bears' stove
day of alleged break-in.

However, despite evidence leaning heavily against Golden Bandit, Bandit stated,

"When the Bears arrived home from their walk in the woods, I feared for my life."

A witness on the prowl confirmed Bandit's accusation stating that he in fact saw Bandit flee from Bears' home, screaming repeated allegations of rape and attempted murder. Bandit's father, a superior court judge stated he would prosecute the Bears to the fullest extent of the law, and signed warrants for their arrest.

Mr. & Mrs. Bear held in Mad-Poly-Trick County Jail, sued Golden Bandit for illegal entry, theft, vandalism, loitering and defamation of character. The Bears also sued for Reparation they claim is due for injustices such as these recurring in their family's history for the past 500 plus years.

Sadly however, Child Protection Services have placed Baby Bear in foster care until courts can further decide whether or not Mr. & Mrs. Bear are fit parents to raise Baby in a safe healthy environment.

That's it for tonight.
This has been the BWYB News saying,

We tell the truth about the Fairies on your tail.

GENTRIFIED BIRD WARNING

Upstairs at
West Oakland Bart
I wait for train when
Pain from above
Nudges my brain

I look up
Little Bird stares down
Asks,

What you looking at?

Balanced between spiked beams says,

You took our trees, homes.
Dare us to live?
Dare us to rest?
Build a nest?
Have a family?
You lie!

We see you ride inside that
Loud fat worm running underground!

You cut away our trees for THAT?!

When our savior
Pterodactyl The Most High returns
He'll suck you out that loud ass maggot
And spit out your bones!
Fuck you!!
I'm here!!!

Turns her back
Attends home
Spikes threatening her life
At every turn

HOW DID I KNOW?

In living room
On floor mat one afternoon
Knapping between worlds
Of the seen and unseen
Birds' crying song
Touches me

I know, I hear you ask
How can one determine
If birds are crying?

If they are indeed crying
By what method of tonal frequency
Could you detect birds' crying song?

I do not know
I cannot tell you

Their refrain awakened me
From what I believed a dream

Though when I opened my eyes
I could still hear them weep
When I stood up

I could still feel their misery
When I opened the door
From the second floor
My eyes were drawn down
Witnessing brown birds
Fluttering wildly
Over lifeless kin on the ground

How did I know
How did I know
Birds' song of sorrow

THE AMERICAN BOTANIST

Botanist travels to South American Rainforest
Seeks to know the mycelium secrets it secretes
What powers of mind it possesses to prophecy
He enters a village where elder's eye his spirit
Tells him of a Shaman that lives deep in the forest

Trekking through dense terrain with
Large flying insects on their own journeys
The botanist confronts a large black iridescent bird
Nearly five feet tall
Standing six or more feet away

He blinks not sure of what he's witnessing
Then sees the Shaman with a dark iridescent feather
Hanging from his long raven black hair he
Gestures the botanist to sit on a fallen log
Shaman pulls mushroom from leather pouch studded
With tiny red beads that form
Pleiades constellation of shapeshifters beginnings

He telepathically conveys to the botanist

Eat of this mushroom amid full moon and
You will find sacred memory of this food

Botanist obeys
Removes red-brown mushroom
Bites chews swallows his ticket
Back to trees' womb
Sways left, right, back, forth,
Descends into roots that spread
In all directions

Art of trees awaken olfactory
Fish womb water flood heart lung
Tympanic drum sings loud
boomBoom, boomBoom, boomBoom, boomBoom
Swoons body into green chlorophyll dream where
Dissonant voice escorts Shaman saying

You monkeys know nothing, nothing, nothing, nothing

Raindrops fall
Head lifts toward light
Soul open
Tears
Run from his eyes

TELL HER

Tell her not to remember
10 years old at daybreak
Mama materializing in her bedroom

Tell her not to remember
How well Mama looked
Dressed in favorite suit
Hair like it had just been done
Walk toward her bed
Bend down and kiss her forehead

Tell her not to remember
Getting up thinking
Mama had come home
From the hospital

Tell her not to remember
Asking 16-year-old cousin
Still in bed clothes where
Mama was, because she
Had just seen her
But couldn't find her

Tell her not to remember
Her cousin look at her and cry

Tell her not to remember noticing time
On kitchen wall read 9:30 AM and
Feel something very bad had happened

Tell her not to remember the ministers coming
To her home later that day
To tell her, "Your Mama has gone home."

Tell her not to remember how she
Paid no attention to that verb variable
As she responded, shaking, scared,

"I know, but I can't find her."

Tell her not to remember
One of the ministers tenderly rephrase,

"We mean she has gone home to heaven."

Tell her not to remember asking
Why God would take Mama
From her and two younger sisters
To live alone with Daddy
Who worked every day

Tell her
30 years later with
Mama's death certificate in hand

Not to remember
Clock on kitchen wall
Read time of death
9:30 AM

Then
Tell her
Spirits can't walk
Without a body

Go ahead
Try
Tell her!

MUTATIONS

Plot, plan, scheme
Game theme
Account

Name
Reason
Rotate season

Interpolate
Isolate
Insert fiction

Alternate
Alternative facts
Inculcate dictums

Connect unknowns
Between elite thrones

Dethrone Isis
Milky Way

Transmogrify
Mutate her say
Domesticate
Sirius
Bitch
Sit heel stay.

IV

Children watch, listen
Dictums stain wonder magic
Hearts of gold grow cold

QUESTIONS FOR SS

I do not feel obliged to believe that the same god who has endowed
us with sense, reason, and intellect, has intended us to forgo its use!

-GALILEO

How old were you when Sunday School
aka SS, told you
God had his only son Jesus
Killed for our sins?
Were you 5, 6, 7 years old?
Did you ask,
What does sin mean?

Did SS answer,
It means you were born broken.

Did you ask why
Seeing you had no broken bones?

Did SS say that your soul was broken!

When you were 10, 11, 12
Did you ask,
What does soul mean?

Did SS answer,
Soul is passion you are not to feel because it belongs to god!

Did you ask,
When did this sin happen to your soul?

Did SS reply,
When Adam and Eve ate from the forbidden
Tree of knowledge, their god forbade them to eat!

Did you ask,
How did sin happen to you if this happened
Before you were born?

Did SS teacher clench his jaw, answering
In a scary low tone through his teeth,
You ask too many questions?

Did he then ask,
Where's your faith?

How did this verbal exchange make you feel?
Did you become asthmatic, confused, or agitated?

As you grew older did you learn
Not to question those in authority?
Did you wonder why you were born?

Did SS try to console you by saying,
God is the glue that will put you together
And forgive you of your sins
If you claim him as your lord and savior?

How did you react when you learned,
Sin in Greek means *to miss the mark*?
Did you wonder what mark you missed?

Did you wonder why god would create you broken?
Then have his only son sacrificed for your sin
To fix the brokenness he created?

Does the church believe in reincarnation?
How is it then that we're born broken?

Why is the bible called the good book
If it tells of god's only son dying for our sins?

Did you ever wonder why god didn't stop
The murder of his only son?

Did you question god's love for his son?

Did SS tell the story of god asking Abraham
To sacrifice his only son, Isaac?

Did you ask SS why god would ask
Abraham to do such a thing to his only son?

Did SS explain that god needed to test Abraham's loyalty to him?

Did god sound like a loving god, or a bully?

Does god want you to love him no matter
How he treats you?
What kind of example is god setting?

How often did SS tell you,
God is love?

Did SS say,
God is good all the time?

Did you consider god a good model for your parents?

Did SS repeatedly tell you,
If you do not accept Jesus as your lord and savior
you will burn in hell for eternity
And not enter the gates of heaven?

Was it enough to look in the night sky
See heaven and make love?

Did you ask why god would cast you into hell
For not believing in his son?

Did SS answer,
Because he loves you?

Did you wonder what love had to do with it?

Did you become suspicious of SS's god's intent?
Did you feel SS's stories cruel, wrong, indifferent?

Did SS tell you,
Lean not unto your own understanding?

Did you stop feeling and start thinking?
Did you stop sensing with your heart and start
Rationalizing with your mind?

Did you feel an emotional disconnect from your soul?
Did you learn psych means soul/light in Latin?
Did SS break you from feeling your soul light?
Did your body feel less alive?
Did life become bleary or unclear?
Were you afraid to trust your insight?

Did the sun look dimmer outside the church doors?
Did you feel conflict between sun-light and SS's son of god?

Did SS tell you sun-light of nature was an idol
And SS's son of god would save you?

Which have you learned we can not live without?

Did you feel a disconnect from the beauty of Nature and
More concerned with the fear of going to hell?

Did it not feel like hell when the KKK, police, and N's
From the hood shot, hanged, lynched or burned a relative
Friend or someone in the community?

Did it remind you of stories SS taught about Jews
Being oppressed by Egyptians?
Did Egyptians really enslave the Jewish people?

Did you learn the Jewish archeologist found that slavery
The Moses story, and 12 tribes wandering the desert
Did not elegantly match stories in the bible?

Did you wonder if the bible is a true historical document?

Did you wonder who wrote the bible, the Romans or Jews?

If Egyptians were the villains in the Old Testament
Who is culturally closer to you?

Who needs to demonize them, or you?
Who needs to destroy your history, integrity?
Who wants access to your land, genetic memory?

Did SS insist you take to heart Luke 14:26
Where Jesus supposedly said,

> *If any man come to me, and hate not his father*
> *mother, wife, children, brethren,*

sisters and even his own life,
He cannot be my disciple?

Hate your own life!
Did you think Jesus was about love?
Were you confused by this buy-bull passage?
What happened to treat neighbor as thyself?
What's up with hating your life or family?

Why would SS teach loyalty to Jesus
And not each other?
What are we witnessing?
Who owns the land?
Who wants the land?
Was this a Roman plan?

Did you know the letter J was invented
By Greeks less than 500 years ago?
Did the Greeks or Romans create Jesus?

How did the names, Jews, Jesus,
His surrogate daddy Joseph, Jerusalem,
James, Jerimiah, Jonah, Jacob, Job, John the Baptist and
The celebration of the Epiphany, in Janus of January
Come to be a 2000 year old god-spell using the letter J?

Was something lost in translation?

Was there another alpha-bet?
What bet was wagered?
What did SS gamble?

Did you learn the German word for fiction is Roman?
Did they tell you the buy-bull was written
By Romans who spoke Greek?
How did a movement like Christianity
Come to exist in a territory indigenous
To illiterate Jews, occupied by Romans
Who spoke Greek?!
Jews wanted the Romans out!

Did Jesus actually say turn the other cheek?
What did that mean?
Take all the ass whoopin' you can then
Render unto Caesar that which is Caesar's?

Did you believe this story?

Did SS tell you the earth is where the devil lives?
Did you care less for the earth because
SS said it's where the devil lives?

Did you hear the 8-year-old girl say,

> *The devil lives in the center of the earth*
> *Where he comes up from down there to trick people?*

Do you you feel you've been tricked?
Do you feel like caring for the devil's home?
Are you in denial of global warming?

Don't sweat the small stuff or Lucifer in the details?

Did you know Lucifer means light?
Is there something coming to the light?

Recall buy-bull verse where Jesus supposedly said,

I come not to bring peace but a sword!

Does SS couple with governments to manufacture
Ownership of land consent?
Is there truly a separation between church and state?
Why are coins and dollar bills engraved with

In God We Trust?

Why are buy-bulls used to swear in U.S. presidents?
Right hand up, left hand down on book of the crown!
Why does the Queen of England own White House property?

What are we observing?
Upon whose land do we live?

Will ignoring the near-genocide of Native Americans
Be permitted as long as one affirms we're blessed and highly favored?

Whose rules, laws, and covenants are we to believe?

Did you question why SS stands for
Sunday school, Social Security, *Schutzstaffel*,
The Nazi Police.

WE COME FROM STARS

An email from a friend shows a picture of Jesus
Nailed to the cross wearing a crown of thorns
Under a thunder and lightning storm

Next picture shows him no longer on the cross
He looks peaceful, chill, with
The Lord's Prayer written beneath him

The words in this prayer strike a profound chord in me as I read

> *Our father who art in heaven*
> *Hallowed be thy name*
> *Thy kingdom come*
> *Thy will be done on earth as it is in heaven*

So I replied

Do you believe in astrology?

I'm asking because the verse in the Lord's Prayer reads

> *Our father who art in heaven*
> *Hallowed be thy name [meaning holy]*
> *Thy kingdom come*
> *Thy will be done on earth as it is in heaven*

Sounds like they believed in astrology

What do you think?

Pardon me? my friend replies
I do believe in the Lord's Prayer
The Bible tells us when we pray
Pray the Our Father which art in heaven, *etc.*

What do *you* pray?
If this is some *thing* you do not believe in
Then I will not include you in my emails
Because I do!

I replied
I understand, but for clarity
Please read *etc.* portion of prayer you negated

> *Our father who art in heaven*
> *Hallowed or (holy) be thy name*
> *Thy kingdom come thy will be done*
> *On earth as it is in heaven*

I wait for a response
Hear nothing back

It has been years

I should have known when

Hallowed be thy name
Thy kingdom come
Thy will be done
On earth as it is in heaven

Was replaced with *etc.*

The Lord's Prayer had no vision
One memorizes prayer but
Cannot see prayer's word

Only rote memory, void of knowledge
Causes heaven to fall from our eyes

FIVE GATES OF HEAVEN

Humanity is seeded from the stars and we have a profound
genetic kinship with humanity's stellar brethren.

–ROD SKENEDORE, NATIVE AMERICAN ELDER

I

Warm summer night
Stardust memory
Birth kin to kitchen
Like puppet
Hand ascends to doorknob
Turns clockwise
Opens new dimensions
Feet step onto balcony
Under big Mama-Papa canopy
Eyes wide upon star jeweled site
I need not die to own heaven's delight

Night Blooming Jasmine signals olfactory
Head bows reverently looks up again
Left hand rest over heart
Right hand lifts
Points inside grandeur of azure luminance
Within milliseconds,

Atop finger tip
Star light blazes across sky

Head bows again.
Why?

What am I to know?
Who forced me out the door?
How did I know
Starlight's time of arrival?

II

Cloaked in midnight
Stars DNA strings seize my body
Pulls head like marionette to sky.

Teapot beings gaze back.
Can they do that?
I can feel them.
Should I know them?
Seems they know me.

The Great Grandmother-Father said
"We are all relatives in this living room."

What do they want of me?
Why can't I remember?
Did churchman warship blast
Stars purpose from memory?

"Shhhhh!," Elder whispers,
"Listen!"

First tell why they haunt me? I ask,
What agency demands I not read
Their deed of trust?

Which Arc?
By whose covenant
Double-crossed my sense-Ori?

III

Who am I
This me in me that
Stares at them twinkling?

What eye in me knows their soul?
What glow sewn to bone does heart see?
Why did copper carbon iron nitrite burst

Pairs in me, breathe breath in me
Clothe a Holy Ghost name in me?

Earth's living waters is my home!
Why have I forgotten lessons of this throne?
Why do tides rise carrying
Missed-trees I cannot hide?

IV

Church fathers say,

> *Star knowledge is sin*
> *Devil's work*
> *Fortune telling*

In secret we learn sin means
To miss the mark
We watch church fathers miss mark often
They have no ledge, footing, or balance
They overlook heaven's fortune
Stars' covenant with earth

We are made of stars
They watch over us

Their celestial rhythm is our rhythm
Stellar instruction feeds us well
Food, soil, grows richer
Water, cleaner

Church fathers tell us,

> *Pray the Our Father*

Why?

You provide no integrity to this prayer's word
On earth as it is in heaven?
Church prayer speaks without deed
Their god-spell has no trust

Churchman tells us,

> *You're not to know how the heavens go*
> *You're to know how to go to heaven*

Their Christ is our crisis
Heaven on earth is our living word

Churchmen talk out their head
Like they want us dead!

V

Churchman's word breaks soul-our light
Forces sun star moon from eyes
Makes heaven fall from sky

Churchman tells us to pray to their father in pair-of-dice
This guesswork gambles with lives that won't survive!

Churchmen tell us,

> *Fall on your knees, let go of legs-that-see*
> *God the father, his son, and ghost*
> *Is all the history you will need*

Church takes land, language, culture, gold, minerals
In spells they call doctrine of discovery by law of a holy see
Make our covenant with heaven and earth, wrong
In judgments we cannot believe

Tell us,

> *The rise of sun's daily light cannot compare*
> *To god's son who died for our sins and rose*
> *From the dead and will return*

Do they not understand our Sun returns every day?
Walks on water, feeds multitudes by season's moon every day?

Church words burn hearts
Dims light
Threatens,

> *If you do not wait for god's son to return*
> *You will commit a sin against church father*
> *And not be saved for heaven when you die!*

We question their lack of honor on Earth
In heaven while alive
If our Mother-Father Sun's light dies
There will be no life!

Church warns again,

> *If you do not have faith*
> *In our father's son and ghost*
> *You will burn in hell for eternity*
> *And be among the antichrist!*

We listen to churchman's god-spells
And submit

If we convert to his warship
We become Anti-life!

SPARROW'S EYE

THREE TIMES IN FIVE DAYS

I

4 / 2 1 / 0 2

One sunny Sunday afternoon
Ascending stairs at
Jack London Square
On to courtyard partially barred
I sit at its pinnacle

By bay this day of heat
My senses drink greedily

Sun walks water
Vault of heaven bright blue
Swaddles family hues
Women men children babies
Eyes laugh talk pleasing
Folks walking easy
Winds blowing breezy

I lift my head toward skies
When suddenly Sparrow

Graces my horizon
Lands right in front of me
Delivers another kind of peace
I feel silent serene

When all at once
Its feathers flutter
My spine tingles, I shudder
Like mirrors
We look directly into one another
And cock our heads to the same side
A moment of unity confides

We stare

We share

Then sparrow flies and flies
With a piece of my light

And Sparrow's in me.

II

4 / 2 4 / 0 2

Three days later
Near my lap's end
Another Sparrow descends

So quick, so near
Without fear, it was as if
Sparrow demanded I stop

So I did
As it hopped from my right to my left
And looked up at me

Must be a kindred spirit I think

Amazed I look down
At this little miracle
On the ground and sense
A heavy release

Feel lighter, a bit more free

Then Sparrow flies and flies
With a piece of my light
And Sparrow's in me.

III

Now the next day
More happens than I wish to say
But Sparrow's theme continues to play

Thursday night open mic
At N'ercity's Blues Joint
I sat listening to poetry and prose

As spoken word neared its close
A woman asked N'er City
If she could sing
So she sang this very old song,

> *I sing because I'm happy*
> *I sing because I'm free*
> *Well, his eyes are on the Sparrow*

And I know Sparrows are watching me

In studies of cultural anthropology
Birds are sign offerings of messages to come

To the Shaman Priest the sparrow means
Desire, fertility of race
The power of song.

SYNCHRONICITY AND THE BIRD

I'm a synchronistic story junkie.
I watch the universe ride alongside
Plants, animal species, and human beings
Merging life into historical mysteries.

Like that Friday in San Francisco when
Late autumn breeze ends poetry
At John Muir Elementary with the
Last child running out the door saying,
"That was fun!"

Tall windows televise gray clouds
Blocking sun's last bit of light.

Keys clang against the door.
It's Marilyn,
Elder Asian who is head custodian.

"It's cold and windy outside.
If you leave now I can lock up," she says.

Sounds good, I answer.
I throw on my long wool coat,

Pick up my book bag and walk
Quickly through the door she locks behind.

We merge into the long hallway of
Students' written work with art displays,
when Marilyn asks,

"How kids doing with poetry this year?"

Which wasn't peculiar having caught her
Many times standing by the door listening,
Smiling or showing concern.

"Let me show you," I say,
Reaching down in my bookbag, that reads
Weaving a Web of Words Around the Tree of Life.
I pull out the California Poets in the Schools anthology entitled
A Wilderness of Dreams.

Just as I'm about to show Marilyn my student's poem,
I see Cecilia, the principal, near the exit.
She notices me and waves to get my attention.

When Marilyn and I reach Cecilia,
I tell Cecilia that my student and I were published
In this year's state anthology.

"Oh really? What did you write?" she asks.
Reaching for the anthology,

Surprised, I hand the book to her,
Thinking her interest would lie
With my student's poem.

"Uh, oh, ok, my poem is entitled
'Holy Ghost' on page 80."

"Ohhh?"
She responds in a long roll,
Eyes wide with wonder as if connecting a mystery.

As she opens the book to my poem.
I begin to recite it from memory.

Cecelia stops reading and listens.
When I finish, Marilyn jumps in.

"I like the way you say that poem. Niiice."
As though the letter 'i' gave it more power.

However, Cecilia appears child-like, mystified.
She had, after all, been a nun before becoming principal.

"How serendipitous it is for me to hear this poem
After all that's happened to me today."

"What happened," I ask, hoping to collect another story.

She immediately engages us on her journey.

Raising her voice, enunciating each word:

"On my way to work this morning,
A bird flew alongside my car for two whole blocks.
Can you believe it?
A whole two blocks!!
And when I stopped,
It stopped.
Landed in front of me on the hood of my car,
Stared me right in my eyes, then flew away."
It was amazing.
I know there was a message there.'"

Cecelia's plump face blushes red pink, as she continues.

"What does it all mean?
And to think October 4th was Saint Francis of Assisi's' birthday.
Today is October 6th.
Birds always flew around him.
He worshipped birds.
He was from Sicily.
My name is Cecilia.
My name comes from Sicily.
Now your poem, 'Holy Ghost'.
What a day."

With arms outstretched as if to look up to an omnipotent being,
She asks once more,

"What does it all mean?"

Weaving a web of words around the tree of life,
We share word-magic in a wilderness of dreams.

How wonderful it is to fly through
Emancipating skies of my poem's insight.

HOLY GHOST

Holy ghost
Where heavens bank
On earth shorelines mothers
Where tides rise and break
By sun moon and stars and
Children come forth
As birthed ships
Profits of immortalities

I said children come forth
As birthed ships
Profits of immortalities

Cells trillions
Singing throughout millenniums
Holding tones laws genes beams
Waiting to astro-blast into
Star life star like generations

Generations germinating
Genii and genies of
Life light blood
Living waters
Captured and held

By wells of human cells
And held prisoner
Of infinite talents
Faiths wisdoms and prophets

Oooh holy ghost mystery
Spooks like a ghost!

Yet organs cling to origin
Play keys
Fulfill wishes
Breathed on banks
And profits the prophet
Of the holy ghost

And profits the prophet
Of the holy ghost

And profits the prophet
Of the holy ghost

SPIRIT SPEAKS

Remember what I told you.
What I whispered in your ear
When I made you face
The sun moon and stars
Reminding you of who we are
My dear one?

Remember how you pleaded
To understand the light that night?
Listening to The Will
That made you stand still
My dear one?
Do you remember?

Do you remember *Annulus Norma*?
Word given which disturbed you
Because you knew not its meaning
But could identify sound origin?

It was Latin.
The only foreign language learned
In nursing school.

Do you remember my dear one?
Do you recall the night you heard
Annulus Norma, Annulus Norma
And what you found them to mean?

Wind, the carpenter square ring
Gauge rule guide law principle
Measure mark of the narrative

Do you remember dear one?

Remember this wheel
Remember this seal
Remember cycles time rhythm rhyme
On paths of mercy and wrath

Every life form is adorned in it
Every life form is born in it

> *Ezekiel saw the wheel*
> *Way up in the middle of the air*
> *Ezekiel saw the wheel*
> *Way in the middle of the air*

CROP CIRCLES

They call it a hoax, a fraud,
There are no extraterrestrials.
Extraterrestrials did not create the crop circles,
Doug and Dave admit they created them all.

Media outlets across the country demonstrate how it was done,
The time it took, the tools they used:
A plank, rope, looped wire, and hats was all.

Really?

Then why did the media refuse to reveal
What renowned scientists have known?

That it would be irrational to think such vast structures
With unfailing detail could be made without days
If not months of delicate labor honoring no footprints
In or out of the crop circles that appear overnight
Within minutes in fields bearing grain trees ice
And flowers left blooming!

Thousands were hidden from public view months before
Doug and Dave's claim to have created them all.

Over ten thousand have been sited
And growing.

Aerial views measure crop circles up to a thousand feet long
Symmetry astounding
Semiology flawless
Concentric circles
Exact diameters
15 to 100 feet wide
Lines joining sunlit circles
Illume ribbons, squares, triangles
Pressed upon combed grains
Braided weave half circles
3, 4, 5, 6, 7, 8, 9 division circles
Unblemished 5, 6, 7, 8, 9, 10 pointed star circles or
409 circles amassing a wheel from hub connecting
Six spokes made of 13 circles, mirroring 2 to 3
Smaller circles down the length of each spoke
Generating right angles waving tips that bend and blend
With yet another spoke in revelry
Of a wheel 780 feet wide or
Two and a half football fields long
Geometrically precise
Not a footprint in sight
Not one grain damaged
Agriculturalist admit yield stronger seed
Producing larger plants than those
Unaffected by crop circles.

Grains stems perfectly bent ninety-degree angles
Exhibit stalks spun clockwise counter-clockwise
Fashioning baskets, octagons, hexagons, pentagons
Made of flowers and grains evenly latticing overlay of stems
Where some look like keys
Constellations planetary orbits faces Ankhs
Calendars and mind fuck wonder
So mathematically and geometrically exact
The ratios reflect micro to macro cosmic disciplines
Within a quarter of an inch.

Doug and Dave did not touch this!

Electrical equipment often fails inside crop circles.
Pets often refuse to go near crop circles
Or their owners that have been inside a new crop circle.

A crop circle witness asked,
"If you think humans created these crop circles
Where are the fields they used for practice?
You'd think landowners that survey their crops regularly
Would notice someone practicing to make a crop circle of this magnitude."

Crop circles appear overnight,
They're ancient metaphysical esoteric and mystical.

Jesus may not have returned, but others definitely have.
Face it, we are not alone.

We're in wondrous times

Which brings to mind Einstein:

The scientist's religious feeling
takes the form of rapturous amazement
at the harmony of natural law,
which reveals an intelligence of such superiority that,
compared with it,
all systematic thinking
of a human mind is seen
as utterly insignificant reflection.

I'm a witness, Baby!
Living in the Twilight Zone, One Step Beyond.

WE DOCUMENT

Hold infinity in the palm of your hand and eternity in an hour.

– WILLIAM BLAKE

We document this day
In prayerful wonder

On earth we kneel
Sun coiling heat around spines
Bridging fingertips play
In Big Mama's clay

Black 6-year-old man-child
Stares into palms vessel as though a
Precious treasure had been found

San Francisco bay salt water scent
Taps leaves
Applauds as

Little one studies

Asks, "What are we made of?"
Turning back his gaze at lump of clay in hand

I say
We are made of ashes, bones, homes, and seed
Dirt, water star memories ancestors left
For us to grow on

They come back through us
That's why G Mama says you look like
Her Grandpa she remembers
From her childhood

He listens
Breathes sweet deep
Shoulders drop relaxes under bright sky

He smiles remembering histories
Known only through his looking glass

Ten-year-old big brother adds with authority

> *And God is not just way up in the sky*
> *God lives with everything*
> *Including our ancestors*
> *With everything above and*
> *Everything below*

"Whoa!"
Little brother says
Eyes marveling from earth-jewel to sky

The whole world in their hands

LIFE ROOTS

Life roots imitate
Mother cells
Mammary wells
Water feeding trees
Fertile water weaves
Sun dipped in fire
Lips with tongues
Weave in tales
Encode in lungs
Behave on behalf
Of memory sung

Flung in wave
Around the world
In all seed
Man woman boy girl
Engraved in tones
Sewn to bones
In each one's temple sternum
Mama poem

Where language sang
Survival arrival in music
Chanted voodoo

Called it hoodoo to blues it
Have you been to the blue?

Certainly Lord
Versed a curse
On earth as it is in heaven
In meters that matter
In 5, 6, & 7

In the DNA
The ground wire was laid
The law is in light
And Amen-Ra raided
Everyone's home
In everyone's bone
Elementing life
In the Mother tongue tone
In the Mother tongue tone
In the Mother tongue tone

MEMORY'S WING

We ride ghostly caverns
Red iron silt
Navel to navel
Ship to shore
Sun light winds win
Tomb to womb
Womb to tomb

Moon tithe nine times
Parting waters in
House of hearts

Reed omnipotent breed
Breathes horns
Born blood memory

Records symphonies
Time without end

Fin feet feather deed seed
Living trust
Magnifying miracles
Hallowed names

Chariots
That let us ride!

STAR JOURNEYS

Mid night cradles dream in
Stardust soul-our memories
Knocks eyes open
        Gliding up third eye

Glow stares back
Saying

We watch you
Take care of you
Cannot let you go
Though you are trained
To let us go

We are your kindred
Kindling purpose in this living room

We keep
Eternal light fires in
And all around you

Have you seen effervescent
Green gold purple pink roll through room?
There is no evil in this knowing

What?
Are you serious?
Are you serious?

Currents buzz head to toe
Hands feet body tingle
Covers I throw
Crawl to window

Who are you?
Who are you?

Isis
Renamed
Sirius
Dog Star

Twinkle, twinkle, little ...

RE-MEMBER

Re-member when stars
Kissed your eyes?
You looked at me
Talked about the
Teapot Constellation in '77
Year of the Snake
Same year that child was born
Re-membering she'd been here before
When she got old enough to explain it

Re-member how she'd reach for her mama
Quick smooth like Orunomamu's snake
Reacting to a sudden gust of wind?

She'd move just like that

Real sensitive that child's ARC-knowledge-tree

Could have birthed more like her in this world
If Noah's Ark deluge story hadn't drowned
So many sacred spines of every kind

But she made it
We made it

Chariot let us ride from the other side
Where redeemers of dreams abide

No
You wouldn't know their names

More than you or I can count

Sealed in eternity's wheel
This little light we shine
We let the vine sign

Who's *we* you ask?
Our cadres from lives past

Hear them?
We do!
They got our back!

V

Red river members
Teach synchronicity's trust
Survive without end

IT'S ON

If a child is born in the era of the 3rd Reich, the child will
be educated for the purposes of the 3rd Reich...

 –JAMES BALDWIN, 1963

Summer of '96 handing out leaflets for a health fair
Regal elder sistah sits in her portable lawn chair
Under a grand magnolia tree
Back straight head held high
Well-groomed wig rests upon her stately chestnut face
Make-up in place she feels my gaze
Turns around gives a quick nod and
Returns to brothers baptizing Nommo Blues on stage
Raising her hand she bows her head in silent testimony
Gives praise to those who know the truth about the blues
Then graces her face back to me nods again cordially
Extending her hand to receive the health fair leaflet
She reads quickly and says

> *Honey, I'm coming to this health fair cause*
> *If we don't start taking care of ourselves*
> *The other folk will*

> *Child, I heard just the other day a neo-Nazi say on the radio*
> *That it is okay to keep Black folk in their place*
> *Yes he did!*

He said, 'We don't need to kill them all
Hitler's example with the Jews took things too far'
That's what that Nazi said, baby

Acid drips dissolving my stomach into a knot as she continues

He said all we need to do is
Take more control of Black folk
Because they've gotten too uppity
Black folk need to be slowed down
He said, 'Black folk want too much'
Did you hear what I said honey?
We better GET prepared so we can BE prepared

This was more than I wanted to hear or understand
I didn't want bad news mixed with the blues
I've got to be positive
Got to have hope
We've come a long way, haven't we?
It's 1996!

I wait patiently for her to finish the Nazi rant and
When she does I respond patronizingly

"I know what you mean
Hope to see you at the health fair"

I smile pleasantly and quickly turn to the next person

Sun shining luminous bright
Blues playing for lovers' eyes
We thrive, right?

Home in bedroom
Summer sunset shadows creep slowly
On my bed like a black cat
Head heavy resists elder's views
About neo-Nazi interview

I collapse flat on my back
Breathe deep release uneasiness inside me
Meditate let go of elder's warning
Drift into sound sleep until
Eyes open with urgency

Ghosts come out my mouth
Like speaking in tongues at church
Spirits all up in this room
Sit me up
Place feet on floor
Turn head like a remote controlled antenna
Accessing a signal then stops
Forces me to stand in the dark
Walk stop and extend my hand
To reach for a tape in a rack of many tapes
I cannot see nor read in the dark

Tape in hand I fumble for light switch to read
What spirit demands and to my surprise the tape cover reads
Neo-Nazi, the Rise

Neo-Nazi, the Rise?
When was this taped?
Did I tape this?

Who stole my memory?
My history?
Telling me I have no evidence
Telling me I'm paranoid
Telling me to forget
Telling me you didn't see like that you saw this
Be positive
Judge not lest I be judged

Who restored the phrase
New World Order?
What devout Christian leader did they get it from?
If we hear see and speak no evil will it go away?

Listen
If a force a will no doubt an ancestor
Olocun deity or some kind of protector
Can wake me from my sleeping state
And guide me through darkness to pick up a tape
Whose subject I tried to escape

The shit is on!

What's happened since 1996?

In 2008 a radio interview with political research journalist Jim Marrs said

> *And again you have all these prominent people in power today,*
> *President of the United States, governor of California, the pope, Karl*
> *Rove, whose grand-father was a Nazi party officials know as Bush's*
> *brain, once removed from the true old Nazis. These are not neo-Nazis.*
> *There is nothing neo or new about them, they're the real guys.*

Memory is an insurance policy against loss
Memory is an insurance policy against loss
Memory is an insurance policy against loss
                              Against loss

PREFACE OF THREE WOMEN

1987, Dr. Frances Cress Wellsing,
Third-generation Black Psychiatrist speaks to a conference
About the use of her Mind's Computer.

> *While walking passed the library, my head kept turning*
> *To a book title displayed in the window.*
> *It was then I knew my mind's computer*
> *Had alerted me to an answer I had been questioning.*

Somebody's watching, somebody cares
Somebody's watching, we can feel it in the air

1990, after Koncepts Cultural Gallery meeting,
Nearing the exit, I'm stopped.
Head turns left,
Looks down at three stacks of newspapers on the ground.
Headlines of no interest,
I step forward again but feel unable to move.

Somebody's watching, somebody cares

Head turns again,
Looks down once more.

This time, eyes stare at stack of papers
Nearest the exit, where it seems
I'm no longer reading headlines that face me.
Instead, I am seeing something my two eyes can not.

Magnetic force suddenly takes my hand downward,
Roots beneath papers,
Pulling out a headline that seals my fate:

White Privilege: Unpacking the Invisible Knapsack of Racism
by Wellesley Professor Peggy McIntosh

> *I was taught to see racism only in individual acts of meanness*
> *not in invisible systems conferring dominance on my group.*

Of the three groups of newspapers,
This is the only issue.

Somebody's watching, somebody cares
Somebody's watching, we can feel it in the air

Witnessing what I've seen in classrooms,
I make copies of the article,
Place it in teachers' boxes.

Over the years I'd hear Peggy McIntosh
On the radio,
Speaking somewhere across the country,
Or I'd watch her on YouTube.

One day, 23 years later,
White Privilege article pinned near my desk
Garners more attention than usual.
I'd review it, put it down and move on.

Days later, walking to the car from Oakland farmer's market,
Facing Oakland Convention Center's large windows,
I see African, Latinx, and Asian children's books on display.

What event is this?
I ask the Native American couple walking out the door.

> *It's a 3-day multicultural conference called NAME,*
> *The National Association of Multicultural Educators.*
> *You should check it out.*

I go in and feel led to an area that displays Freedom Lifted posters.
The vendor directs me to a table
Where my eyes immediately zoom in on
Powder-blue folder labeled
'The Privilege Conference."
I pick it up to examine.

Vendor working the table asks,

> *Have you heard of this conference?*

Only as it relates to an article read years ago titled
White Privilege Unpacking the Invisible Knapsack of Racism.

Yes, that'd be the one. I believe Peggy McIntosh is still here.

Here?

Yes, she spoke a little while ago.

Where?

Vendor gives directions to Peggy's table.
As I begin my trek toward her, I realize
I don't have a clue what she looks like,
And didn't think to ask.

Somebody's watching, somebody cares

I keep walking pass vendor displays.
No one looks like Peggy McIntosh to me.
I expect a hipster woman dressed New Age.

I ask a friend I see if she knows Peggy McIntosh.
Said she didn't but could direct me to someone who might,
Introduces me to a producer of seldom-seen
Documentaries on Civil Rights.

After our exchange, I ask him if he knows
Peggy McIntosh.

> *Yes! I sure do.*
> *She looks like Santa Clause's wife*

if you can picture that.
I believe she's still here.
Her table is on this side of the aisle.

Thank you.

I hurry down the aisle, when my eyes
Instantly engage his description, reading a book.

Dang, she does look like Santa's wife.
Soft tears form.
Why?

Are you Peggy McIntosh?

Yes I am.

I have been distributing your article
White Privilege for years.
It's an honor to meet you.

> *Why are you so honored?*
> *You know this information already don't you?*

Yes, I do, but I wasn't looking for it.
Your article presented itself to me.

Tilting her head, she squints her eyes.

Was your experience otherworldly?

Yes it was.

Do you have time to sit with me?

It's why I'm here.

I walk to the other side of the table
Where a chair awaits me.

Interesting your experience being
Otherworldly. Tell me what happened.

I explain how my hand was magnetically drawn
Underneath a stack of papers
For an article I couldn't see, and how
Hers was the only one in the pile I withdrew.

She then tells me

I was accused of being a racist.
Couldn't believe it.
Considered myself and other Whites I respect
Nice people.

When White men, though nice and polite, denied
Women's Studies for first year undergrads,
Calling it extracurricular,

That's when the alarm sounded for me.
How can your mother, sister, or wife, be extra anything?

I asked for truth to be revealed,
Prayed in earnest.
Couldn't believe what I was shown.
Because I thought I was a good White woman,
Not a racist.
However, I've learned that thinking you're nice
Is not synonymous with behavior.

In 1987, Dr. Frances Cress Welsing confirmed
That use of the Mind's Computer alerted her
Of answers to that which she questioned.

In 1990, my body was magnetically drawn
To Peggy McIntosh's article, *White Privilege,*
Unconscious of what I would be unpacking.

And in 2013, I'm drawn
To a conference of which I am unaware,
Meet Peggy McIntosh in person, and
Listen to her otherworldly education, using dreams,
While our collective realities witness

Somebody's watching, somebody cares
Somebody's watching, we can feel it in the air

IF I HADN'T

If I hadn't run in circles when 3-years-old on fields of
grass with Black Bird chasing me or me chasing it,

If I hadn't remembered recurring dream at 7 years of age, swallowing
small stones, choking under bright lit sky in front of a long dark
tunnel, holding pinpoint light; if an Ethiopian woman hadn't
interpreted my dream recognizing an old saying from her culture,

If my body hadn't heaved and cried that day in 1989, recalling what
happened 17 years prior with a chemistry professor who said
I could not use the problem solving methods of Africans with whom
I studied because they were going back to Africa; I was not,

If I hadn't learned PTSD & PTSS are body's cognitive
ability to record and remember pain,

If I hadn't experienced migraines while studying for three exams,
looking for subject-connectedness within a circle, reading a book
given to me, titled Muntu, and find a quote that read, "For the
African, to disengage one subject from life's circle would paralyze
the rest," and have migraines disappear shortly thereafter,

If I hadn't been haunted by small globular lights, Van Allen's belts—
solid gold, lime, purple spheres amassing iridescent lights that would
suddenly appear, and learn inter-dimensional beings do exist,

If I hadn't been awakened by a tiger watching me calmly
in dream, heard a spirit come down the roof through the
ceiling, and feel its weighted impression beside me,

If I hadn't called and talked to a Zen Buddhist priest for 2
hours, who assured me I was not going mad or crazy, nor had I
committed a sin, but was merely entering my enlightenment,

If I hadn't commissioned my astrology chart to be calculated 5 times,
aligning on earth as it is in heaven, as an active noun verb agreement system,

If I hadn't recognized, while studying organic and inorganic chemistry,
that iron is not only a common element found in the body but throughout
the universe, causing life to be pulled or repelled in some way,

If I hadn't attended the Berkeley Psychic Institute, learned how one can
absorb another's programming, been invited to Stanford's Parapsychology
Department with BPI, and discovered a trans-medium who allowed
a spirit to share her body, then discovered another at my job,

If I hadn't seen a slug-sized, lip-suctioning leech, undulating
around a relative's head as though looking for a place to land; and
when it did, weeks later, said relative could not lift her head,

If I hadn't suggested she go to a Chinese acupuncturist, who told her
at the end of the examination, "It's as though something has sucked
the life force from her head," which left me questioning what I saw,

If I hadn't read, in *The Archeology of Knowledge*, "We must also ascribe
to the institutional sites from which the doctor makes his discourse,"

If I hadn't worked in a mental institution as a lab tech and
learned the difference between a psychic and a sick psychic,

If I hadn't heard the birds' crying-song while knapping, unable to
discern how I knew their cry, only to get up, open the door and
see birds fluttering wildly over their lifeless friend, adored,

If I hadn't heard a helicopter in Oakland fly over my house and
drop something on the house at the corner that sounded like a loud
SWOOSH, on May 13, 1985, after 2 AM, on the West Coast,

If I hadn't read in the newspaper later the same morning that
a helicopter dropped a bomb on the MOVE organization's
house on the corner of Osage & Pine in Philadelphia, on the
East Coast at 5 AM, and noted the 3-hour time difference,

If I hadn't felt a patient's medication for his right eye
land as if a web on my left eye, as discovered in his chart
and associated molecular isomers, mirroring molecules,

If I hadn't heard an unknown Goddess whisper in my ear, yet
was shown the spelling of her name in my mind's eye,

If I hadn't found her name in the dictionary, as shown, and learn
she was the deity of love and war, my sun & rising sign,

If I hadn't seen rainbows near sun in clear skies, as if to illume answers
of questioned insight,

If I hadn't been pulled outside to bow my head, point to the vastness
of the night sky, and at the tip of my finger have a shooting star arrive,

If I hadn't awakened abruptly from a deep sleep to see Isis, known
as Sirius, watching over me,

If I hadn't heard a voice say, "You have fidelity in the law and it will
be used as your trench!"

I might not have learned that the Dogons of West Africa, once every 50
years, parade the reflection of star Amma B around A, wearing head-dresses
that resemble telephone poles, because their eyes have not been corrupted,

Or that the African, Chinese, Irish, Cherokee, and Black Foot
understanding of stars in me is on earth as it is in heaven,

And that the experiences, testimonies, visions, and synchronicities
of blood memory I continue to speak have earned me the name
I am today, *D'Jeli Musa*, Story Medicine Woman of Truths,

I may not have recognized an ancestor saying,

> *I come from Mystics*
> *who believe in hearing the inaudible,*
> *touching the intangible and*
> *seeing the invisible.*

Little light shine bright
Wish brings enormous insight
Love, be love, abide.

CLASSROOM GUIDE

Use this book to look at the biology, etymology, senses, and political and religious inferences of language. Remember "The Logical Song" by Supertramp, which speaks to how we are taught not to have magical realism in our lives; how are are sent away to school to be logical, practical, cynical, to do away with endless possibilities and infinite imagination. My hope is that *Synchronicity: The Oracle of Sun Medicine* will unlock the innate possibilities contained within yourself and your students in order to foster more creative approaches and outcomes. What does it mean to let go and trust that the universe will catch us, that will we catch ourselves?

SATIRE, QUESTIONING, CRITICAL THINKING

Humor is a useful tool to ease the burden of what can be so heavy in life. It is important to use the tools of active questioning and critical thinking to peel back the facades and interrogate the scaffolding or dicta imprinted on our psyches.

Below are just a few poems from the book to use in exploring these topics:

- Worship Warship
- Communion
- Questions for SS
- We Come from Stars
- Forgive Us
- If I Hadn't

THE ROLE OF LANGUAGE IN SOCIETY AND CULTURE

Language frames our universe, creating labyrinths, puzzles, and concepts that we often grapple with throughout life.

Below are just a few poems from the book to use in exploring the role of language in society and culture:

- Poly-Tics
- Five Gates of Heaven
- Spell's Labyrinth: Double Talk
- Concept's Philosophy
- Steal Away Baptist Church

CONTEMPORARY COLONIZING AND ABUSES OF POWER

What entitlements have you been told to accept? What entitlements have you been given? Colonizing language—nothing new—usurps land, vision, understanding, and our ability to be cognizant and present. The gossamer third eye, the false frame tricks us and prevents us from being able to envision beyond what has already been envisioned for us.

Below are just a few poems from the book to use in exploring the themes of contemporary colonizing and abuses of power:

- Concept's Philosophy
- BWYB News: The Goldilocks Cover Up
- Take Me Home Mama

- A Moment of Silence
- Today in Oaktown
- Devil's Advocate
- Hidden Agendas
- Gentrified Bird Warning

ORGANIZED RELIGION AND SECULAR FELLOWSHIP/COMMUNITY

How has organized religion stolen your familial history, language, and culture? How has it divided us in the past? How does it divide us now? What does it mean to be in community?

Below are just a few poems from the book to use in exploring these themes and questions:

- Worship Warship
- Questions for SS
- My Sun
- My People
- Look at Her
- Forgive Us

NATURE AND CAPITALISM

When were you told to forgo the immediacy of your visceral, cognitive environment? When were you taught to doubt yourself and your inner nature and innate resilience? Locate your magic.

Below are just a few poems from the book to use in exploring these themes and questions:

- The American Botanist
- Heathens Speak
- Sparrow's Eye
- We Document
- My Sun
- Holy Ghost
- Re-Member

CULTURAL XENOPHOBIA AND HOW HISTORY IS TAUGHT/LEARNED

The prefix "Histo" comes from the Greek word "Histos" meaning web or tissue. Inevitably connected in our beingness, for whom is history written, and how? How might we upend the framing of "the Other" and continue to take up the mantle of telling our own stories?

Below are just a few poems from the book to use in exploring these themes and questions:

- Heathen Speaks
- Take Me Home Mama
- Life Light Remembered
- Nae Nae Tweaks Out On Racist Insult
- Eyes So Bright: Blues
- Holy Ghost

SYNCHRONICITY, STARS, AND CONNECTIVITY

When did you begin to notice patterns reflected in experiences that offered answers to questions or concerns? Have you ever felt drawn to take in the night sky? Have you ever contemplated your relationship to a particular constellation? What cultural references guide you through the night sky?

Below are just a few poems from the book to use in exploring these themes and questions:

- Synchronicity and the Bird
- It's On
- Preface of Three Women
- Five-to-Six-Hundred Years Old
- Five Gates of Heaven
- If I Hadn't

ACKNOWLEDGEMENTS

Big thank you to honored ancestors: Toni Morrison, Amiri Baraka, Orunomamu, Sister MaKinya, and the human family for allowing me to articulate the stage, about which I am still in shock and awe; Nomadic Press Executive Director, J. K. Fowler, and Associate Editor, Michaela Mullin; the Sun family, ancestors, and all who brought us this moment, to bear witness to the synchronistic stories that reveal the seal that heals and sustains future blood memory; my daughter, Thylon Sizemore, an outstanding comedian and major ongoing influence in my life—having her made me a witness to the effects of education systems on all of us; Ted Pontiflet, mentor, whose wit and character never ceases to amaze me; Sheebah Twelde, for offering emotional connectedness to African languages, and opening up environments not seen in English; Professor Ngũgĩ wa Thiong'o for sharing the understanding of how one learns cerebrally under colonialism, rather than emotionally, and thereby naming me *Word Magician*; Al Young, CA Poet Laureate Emeritus, for calling me out at the 16th Annual Poetry Festival in Berkeley; James Garrett, for his encouragement and taking the time to write such an exquisite foreword for this book; Professor Judy Juanita, for encouraging me to write more and publish; Genny Lim, astounding poet who calls out the BS for what it is; James Cagney, godson of immense talent and humor (like dust we rise, and congrats again on winning the 2019 PEN Jospehine Miles Award!); Tongo Eisen-Martin, for support and continuously displayed genius (and thanks to Judy, Genny, James Cagney, and Tongo for writing such satirical wickedly defiant, heartwarming, and insightful blurbs); Dr. Raina J. León, for MoAD, and all around preciousness.

To all those who continue to feed the spirit and support: Elilta Tewelde,

Nazelah Jamison, Tarika Lewis, Jeneé Darden, Avotcja of KPOO and KPFA, Kentake Neal, David and PJ Sykes, Tree of Life Foundation HLP, Michael Orange, Matatu Festival, and Saul Williams, Tea Roots Foundation, The Maroons, The Lower Bottom Playaz, Black Arts Movement, Digital Papers, Marcus Books, and the EastSide Arts Alliance.

Finally, and infinitely, to all community activists, griots/storytellers, artists, film producers, writing workshop presenters, dancers, musicians, and healers in our communities too numerous to mention.

Thank you to the following publications, where some of these poems were previously published, in earlier versions: *Black Gold –The Anthology*, "Five-to-Six-Hundred-Years Old"; *Civil Liberties 2019*, "Life Light Remembered"; *UCB Digital Papers Zine*, "BWYB News: The Goldilocks Cover Up," "Sparrow's Eye," "Re-Member"; *California Poets in the Schools State Anthology*, "Holy Ghost"; *Anacua Literary Arts Journal*, "Heathens Speak"; *DrumVoices Revue, Southern Illinois University—Twenty Year Anniversary*, "Spell's Labyrinths"; *Temba Tupu (Walking Naked!) The Africana Woman's Poetic Self-Portrait*, "Look at Her"; and *New Jersey: Africa World Press*, "Life Roots."

Educator, consultant, poet, griot/elocutionist/story medicine woman, **TUREEDA MIKELL** began working the healing arts in 1977 via poetry, storytelling, and QiGong energy therapy. Mikell is the founder of Tree of Life Health Literacy Project and works in collaboration with California Poets in the Schools. In 2018, Mikell was the Eth-Noh-Tec NuWa Delegate from the US to Beijing, China, in Gengcun Village of renowned storytellers in collaboration with the University of Beijing on mission to heal cultural boundaries. Mikell has been a featured reader with Kim Shuck, Poet Laureate of San Francisco, California, presented Al Young (named poet laureate of California in 2015) with the lifetime achievement award at the 2018 Berkeley Poetry Festival, and has opened for Saul Williams at Grand Lake Theater in Oakland. She is a BAWP Fellow at UC Berkeley's Graduate School of Education, has worked and read with the late Amiri Baraka via EastSide Arts Alliance, and is one of the co-founders of the Black Writers Conference in Otisville, New York. *Synchronicity: The Oracle of Sun Medicine* is her first full-length collection of poetry.

MORE PRAISE FOR

SYNCHRONICITY
THE ORACLE OF SUN MEDICINE

Read *Synchronicity: The Oracle of Sun Medicine* sitting down. It ain't for the faint of heart:

"You want to lay down sword and shield by the Riverside,
While shot, lynched, butchered, burned waft the air?"

Not only will Tureeda not lay down her sword, but her words are her weapons. These poems are a powerful act of exorcism and resistance against white racism and the violence it wields. Tureeda calls out the racist demons of Black history through her rant, cant, and naming of their multiple, evil disguises by her use of puns like *Buy-Bull* for Bible, *profits* for prophets, *prey* for pray, *perish* for parish, and *Son* for Sun, which were key in the conversion of Sun and Nature worshippers into Jesus followers. By exposing the ambiguity and double talk embedded in the Christian language of oppression, Mikell seeks to demystify its cult of "cannibalism," which took the *"Bantu tongue, Ripped into a thousand pieces, Babbles on and on"* in a plea to return to the Native ways. The arc of the book follows Mikell's own journey to healing the broken circle within herself, her community, and in the world without, through angry catharsis to self-reflection and self-reconciliation. In the final chapter, it's the intimate connections Mikell forms with people and nature that are the light and oracles of her *Sun Medicine*.

GENNY LIM

winner of the 1981 American Book Award, American poet
(author of *Winter Place*, 1989, Kearny Street Workshop Press),
playwright, and performer